SHARK FRENZY

Sand Tiger Sharks

by Thomas K. Adamson

BLASTOFF! READERS 3

BELLWETHER MEDIA • MINNEAPOLIS, MN

Blastoff! Readers are carefully developed by literacy experts to build reading stamina and move students toward fluency by combining standards-based content with developmentally appropriate text.

Level 1 provides the most support through repetition of high-frequency words, light text, predictable sentence patterns, and strong visual support.

Level 2 offers early readers a bit more challenge through varied sentences, increased text load, and text-supportive special features.

Level 3 advances early-fluent readers toward fluency through increased text load, less reliance on photos, advancing concepts, longer sentences, and more complex special features.

★ **Blastoff! Universe**

Reading Level

Grade
K

Grades
1-3

Grade
4

This edition first published in 2021 by Bellwether Media, Inc.

No part of this publication may be reproduced in whole or in part without written permission of the publisher. For information regarding permission, write to Bellwether Media, Inc., Attention: Permissions Department, 6012 Blue Circle Drive, Minnetonka, MN 55343.

Library of Congress Cataloging-in-Publication Data

Names: Adamson, Thomas K., 1970- author.
Title: Sand tiger sharks / by Thomas K. Adamson.
Description: Minneapolis, MN : Bellwether Media, Inc., [2021] | Series: Blastoff! Readers: Shark frenzy | Includes bibliographical references and index. | Audience: Ages 5-8 | Audience: Grades 2-3 | Summary: "Simple text and full-color photography introduce beginning readers to sand tiger sharks. Developed by literacy experts for students in kindergarten through third grade"-Provided by publisher.
Identifiers: LCCN 2020001646 (print) | LCCN 2020001647 (ebook) | ISBN 9781644872499 (library binding) | ISBN 9781681037127 (ebook)
Subjects: LCSH: Sand tiger shark–Juvenile literature.
Classification: LCC QL638.95.O3 A33 2021 (print) | LCC QL638.95.O3 (ebook) | DDC 597.3/4–dc23
LC record available at https://lccn.loc.gov/2020001646
LC ebook record available at https://lccn.loc.gov/2020001647

Editor: Rebecca Sabelko   Designer: Kathleen Petelinsek

Printed in the United States of America, North Mankato, MN.

Table of Contents

What Are Sand Tiger Sharks?

coral reef

Sand tiger sharks live in oceans all over the world. These sharks swim in coastal waters near **coral reefs** and rocky bottoms.

4

They are called sand tiger sharks because they **lurk** near the sandy ocean floor.

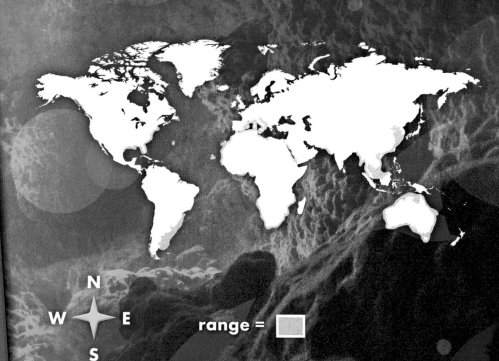

Sand Tiger Shark Range

N
W E
S

range = ⬜

The sand tiger shark population is in danger. These sharks only have one or two babies every two years. They do not have enough young to keep up with fishing.

Some countries have banned fishing for sand tigers to help grow their numbers.

Toothy Grins

snout

Sand tiger sharks have pointed **snouts**. Their wide mouths extend behind their eyes.

Pointy teeth stick out of their mouths in all directions. The teeth jab fish before the sharks swallow them whole.

Sand tigers are almost 18 feet (5.5 meters) long. Two **dorsal fins** sit atop their long bodies.

Shark Sizes

average human

sand tiger shark

- - - 6 feet (2 meters) long

almost 18 feet (5.5 meters) long

dorsal fins

notch

lobe

Their tail fins have a long upper **lobe**. Unlike many other sharks, sand tiger sharks have **notched** tail fins.

The coloring of sand tiger sharks acts as **camouflage**. Their backs match the sandy ocean floor. Their bellies are white.

Identify the Sand Tiger Shark

notched
tail fin

pointed
snout

pointy
teeth

The sharks also have spots.
But these fade as the sharks
get older.

Hovering Hunters

During the day, sand tiger sharks stay near caves and cliffs. They become active at night.

Sometimes these sharks hunt together. They surround **schools** of fish. They drive **prey** to **shallow** waters where it is easy to attack.

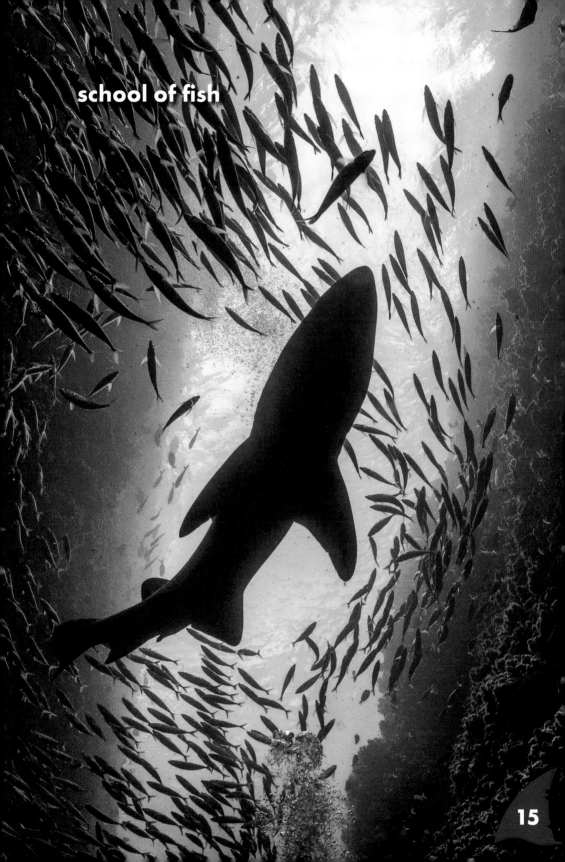

school of fish

Sand tiger sharks also hunt alone.
They swim to the surface to gulp air.
They hold air in their bellies.

This allows them to **hover** in the water as they look for small fish, young sharks, and stingrays.

Sand Tiger Shark Diet

fish

young sharks

stingrays

Young sand tiger sharks are sometimes eaten by larger sharks. But adults have no natural **predators**.

These **carnivores** are top predators of the ocean floor!

Deep Dive on the Sand Tiger Shark

notched tail fin

LIFE SPAN:
up to 35 years

LENGTH:
almost 18 feet
(5.5 meters) long

WEIGHT:
up to 350 pounds
(159 kilograms)

DEPTH RANGE:
0 to 625 feet (0 to 191 meters)

pointed snout

pointy teeth

| Least Concern | Near Threatened | Vulnerable | Endangered | Critically Endangered | Extinct in the Wild | Extinct |

conservation status: critically endangered

Glossary

camouflage—a way of using color to blend in with surroundings

carnivores—animals that only eat meat

coral reefs—structures made of coral that usually grow in shallow seawater

dorsal fins—the fins at the top of a sand tiger shark's back

hover—to wait in one place without moving

lobe—a part of a sand tiger shark's tail

lurk—to stay hidden while getting ready to attack

notched—related to a V-shaped cut in sand tiger shark tails

predators—animals that hunt other animals for food

prey—animals that are hunted by other animals for food

schools—groups of fish

shallow—not deep

snouts—the noses of some animals

To Learn More

AT THE LIBRARY

Alderman, Christine Thomas. *Sand Tiger Sharks.*
Mankato, Minn.: Black Rabbit Books, 2020.

Pembroke, Ethan. *The Shark Encyclopedia for Kids.*
Minneapolis, Minn.: Abdo Publishing, 2021.

Skerry, Brian. *The Ultimate Book of Sharks: Your
Guide to these Fierce and Fantastic Fish.* Washington,
D.C.: National Geographic, 2018.

ON THE WEB

FACTSURFER

Factsurfer.com gives you
a safe, fun way to find
more information.

1. Go to www.factsurfer.com.

2. Enter "sand tiger sharks" into the search box
   and click 🔍.

3. Select your book cover to see a list
   of related content.

Index

The images in this book are reproduced through the courtesy of: Peter Pinnock/ Getty, front cover; Dirk van der Heide, pp. 3, 6-7, 11; imageBROKER/ Alamy, pp. 4-5; Nature Picture Library/ Alamy, pp. 6, 9, 13 (pointy teeth), 21 (pointy teeth); Michael Patrick O'Neill/ Alamy, pp. 8-9, 20-21; Steve Woods Photography/ Getty, pp. 12-13, 22; Pommeyrol Vincent, p. 13 (sand tiger); Stefan Pircher, p. 14 (inset); saulty72, pp. 14-15; Cultures Creative (RF)/ Alamy, pp. 16-17; Al McGlashan, p. 17 (fish); Sekundator, p. 17 (young sharks); StudioSmart, p. 17 (stingrays); Helmust Corneli/ Alamy, p. 18; Tomas Kotouc, pp. 18-19.